Contents

What is Easter?

Easter is a **Christian** holiday. Christians believe that Jesus Christ is the Son of God. They celebrate the day that Jesus was **resurrected**, or came back to life. Easter comes on different Sundays every year. It always falls between March 21 and April 25.

● Children wake up on Easter morning to find treats.

DID YOU KNOW?

Look at a calendar. Find the first full moon after March 21. Now find the first Sunday after that full moon. You found Easter Sunday!

Celebrations in My World

Easter

Lynn Peppas

Crabtree Publishing Company

www.crabtreebooks.com

Crabtree Publishing Company

www.crabtreebooks.com

Author: Lynn Peppas
Coordinating editor: Chester Fisher
Series and project editor: Penny Dowdy
Editor: Adrianna Morganelli
Proofreader: Crystal Sikkens
Project editor: Robert Walker
Production coordinator: Katherine Berti
Prepress technicians: Katherine Berti, Ken Wright
Project manager: Kumar Kunal (Q2AMEDIA)
Art direction: Dibakar Acharjee (Q2AMEDIA)
Cover design: Tarang Saggar (Q2AMEDIA)
Design: Ritu Chopra (Q2AMEDIA)
Photo research: Farheen Aadil (Q2AMEDIA)

Photographs:
123RF: Alexey Bannykh: p. 18; Paul Cowan: p. 24
Alamy: Friedrich Stark / Alamy: p. 31; Steve Skjold: p. 25
AP Photo: Ron Edmonds: p. 23
BigStockPhoto: Ints Vikmanis: p. 5
Corbis: David Barnet/Illustration Works: p. 6; Martin Harvey/
    Gallo Images: p. 30
Dreamstime: Dave Howe: p. 10
Getty Images: Joe Kohen: p. 26; Steve Shott: p. 19; Travel Ink: p. 27
Istockphoto: Miroslava Arnaudova: p. 11; Sharon McIntyre: p. 16;
    Quavondo Nguyen: p. 21; Nicole S. Young: p. 4
Hrana Janto: p. 13
Jupiter Images: Jose Luis Pelaez Inc: p. 1; Kelly Redinger: p. 9
Reuters: Darren Staples: p. 22
Rex Features: p. 28; SNAP: p. 29
Shutterstock: p. 12; Hallgerd: p. 15; Petr Jilek: front cover
    (background); Pawel Kielpinski: p. 8; ncn18: front cover (eggs);
    Thomas M Perkins: front cover (main image), p. 17; Dan
    Riedlhuber: p. 7; Ekaterina Starshaya: p. 14

Library and Archives Canada Cataloguing in Publication

Peppas, Lynn
    Easter / Lynn Peppas.

(Celebrations in my world)
Includes index.
ISBN 978-0-7787-4289-0 (bound).--ISBN 978-0-7787-4307-1 (pbk.)

    1. Easter--Juvenile literature. I. Title.
II. Series: Celebrations in my world

GT4935.P46 2009   j394.2667   C2009-900940-4

Library of Congress Cataloging-in-Publication Data

Peppas, Lynn.
    Easter / Lynn Peppas.
        p. cm. -- (Celebrations in my world)
    Includes index.
    ISBN 978-0-7787-4307-1 (pbk. : alk. paper) -- ISBN 978-0-7787-4289-0
(reinforced lib. bdg. : alk. paper)
    1. Easter--Juvenile literature. I. Title. II. Series.

BV55.P385 2009
263'.93--dc22

                                2009005715

Crabtree Publishing Company

www.crabtreebooks.com   1-800-387-7650

Published in Canada
Crabtree Publishing
616 Welland Ave.
St. Catharines, ON
L2M 5V6

Published in the United States
Crabtree Publishing
PMB16A
350 Fifth Ave., Suite 3308
New York, NY 10118

Published in the United Kingdom
Crabtree Publishing
White Cross Mills
High Town, Lancaster
LA1 4XS

Published in Australia
Crabtree Publishing
386 Mt. Alexander Rd.
Ascot Vale (Melbourne)
VIC 3032

Many Christians go to
church on Easter Sunday.

The Story of Jesus

Jesus Christ lived over two thousand years ago in Israel. Some people did not believe Jesus was the Son of God. They ordered him to be **crucified**, or killed on a cross.

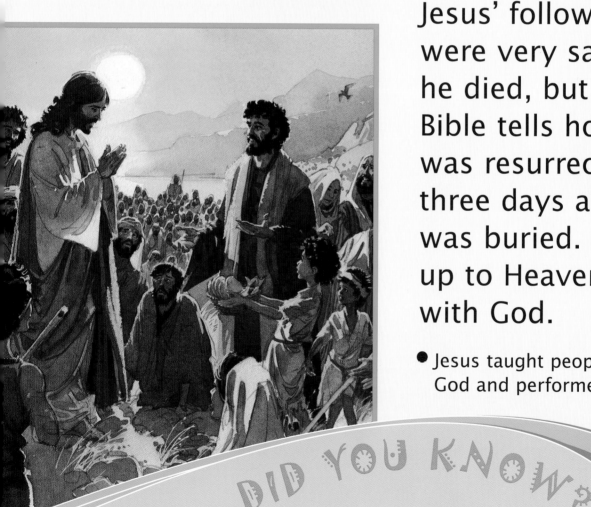

Jesus' followers were very sad when he died, but the Bible tells how Jesus was resurrected three days after he was buried. He rose up to Heaven to live with God.

- Jesus taught people about God and performed miracles.

DID YOU KNOW?

Jesus' story was written almost two thousand years ago. The New Testament of the Bible tells about his life.

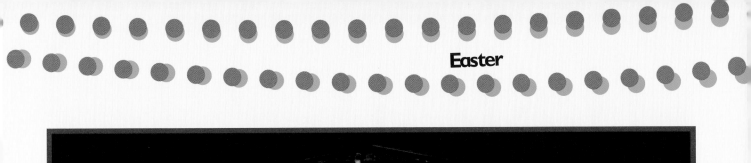

This stained glass window in a church shows Jesus crucified.

Holy Week

Holy Week is the week before Easter. Holy Week begins on Palm Sunday. The Thursday of Holy Week is called Maundy Thursday. On this day Jesus shared the **Passover** meal with his **disciples**. This is called the Last Supper. The next day is Good Friday, when Jesus died on the cross.

• Many Christians go to church during Holy Week to remember the events that led up to Jesus' resurrection.

DID YOU KNOW?

Forty days before Easter, on Ash Wednesday, Christians begin Lent. During Lent, people give up something they like until Easter arrives.

People threw palm branches on the road in front of Jesus to honor him on Palm Sunday.

The Birth of Spring

Long ago, people celebrated spring's arrival. People were happy because spring brought warm weather. Plants and flowers grew again. Animals gave birth. Families could again plant crops. People held feasts and gave each other gifts to celebrate spring.

After Jesus was born, the Christian church kept the spring festival **traditions**. The spring festivals celebrate the rebirth of the land. Easter celebrates the rebirth of Jesus.

DID YOU KNOW?

In North America, Easter occurs in spring. In other countries, Easter falls during autumn.

Baby animals, such as this lamb, are a sure sign of spring!

Goddess of Spring

Long ago, people thought that gods controlled the seasons. People did not grow food during the cold winter months. Some plants lost their leaves. Other plants looked dead. People held festivals to make the gods happy. People hoped their god of spring would bring life to Earth again.

Some believed that the goddess Eostre brought spring to Earth. People held a festival for her when spring came.

● Hares, such as this one, are larger than rabbits and have bigger ears.

DID YOU KNOW?

Eostre's favorite animal was the hare. A hare looks like a rabbit, and looks like the Easter Bunny of today.

People held a special festival to honor this goddess, Eostre.

Symbols of Easter

Easter celebrates the return of life, for Jesus and Earth. People use **symbols** to remember what Easter means. The egg has always reminded people of new life. Baby animals, such as chicks and lambs, stand for new beginnings of life, too. The cross is an Easter symbol as well. It stands for Jesus' death. Christians believe that Jesus died on the cross. Then God forgave peoples' **sins**, or wrongdoings.

● Eggs stand for new life because birds and some animals hatch from them.

DID YOU KNOW?

White lilies, called Easter lilies, decorate homes and churches during Easter.

Easter lilies and the cross are symbols of Easter.

Easter Eggs

Decorating eggs is an old tradition. Eggs can be dyed, or painted. People from different **cultures** decorate their eggs in different ways. In North America, people cook the eggs before coloring them. Then they draw on the eggs with crayons. They put the eggs in colored liquid. The liquid does not color the wax from the crayons, so the design stays on the eggs.

● Ukrainian Easter eggs have beautiful designs drawn on with beeswax.

DID YOU KNOW?

Ukrainian Easter eggs are called Pysanky. Artists draw designs on an egg with beeswax. Then they dye the egg with different colors.

Some people use food
coloring to dye eggs.

The Easter Bunny

Children from around the world wake up excited on Easter morning. It is time to look for the Easter eggs and candy that the Easter Bunny hid. The Easter Bunny has no **religious** connection to Jesus. This tradition started during the ancient spring festivals.

Do rabbits lay candy eggs? No! They have baby rabbits, and usually a lot of them! This is why rabbits and the Easter Bunny stand for new life.

● The Easter Bunny paints designs on Easter eggs.

DID YOU KNOW?

Most people call baby rabbits bunnies, but the real name for them is kittens.

Rabbits can have five to eight kittens in a litter.

Easter Egg Hunt

No one knows when children went on the first Easter egg hunt, but we know that they hunted for eggs during spring festivals. Today, the Easter Bunny hides eggs and treats on Easter morning. Other people have their own egg hunts before or after Easter. Children find different kinds of Easter eggs on egg hunts. Some are real eggs that have been decorated. Others are made of chocolate and wrapped in pretty foil. Sometimes plastic eggs are filled with candies and small toys.

DID YOU KNOW?

*Some Easter eggs make noise so that **visually-challenged** children can find them.*

When you go on an Easter egg hunt, bring a basket to carry the eggs you find.

Easter Games

Children may play games on Easter Monday. Easter Monday is a holiday in many countries such as Canada. It is not a holiday in the United States. One game played on Easter Monday is egg rolling. Children roll their eggs along the ground. They race toward a finish line. In the United States, the president holds an Easter Egg Roll every year at the White House.

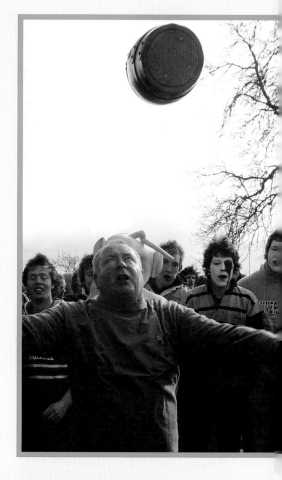

● Easter Monday is a day to play games.

DID YOU KNOW?

People play egg-tapping at Easter. They tap the ends of their hard-boiled Easter eggs together and say "Christ has risen." The player with an unbroken shell wins.

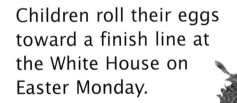

Children roll their eggs
toward a finish line at
the White House on
Easter Monday.

Easter Foods

People eat more than eggs and candy at Easter. In many homes, families cook a special meal. In North America, people eat ham for Easter dinner. Christians also eat lamb for their Easter meal. In the Bible, people **sacrificed**, or killed, lambs as a gift to God. The lamb also stands for Jesus. He is called the Lamb of God.

● Hot cross buns have white crosses on top.

DID YOU KNOW?

Hot cross buns are a traditional food that is eaten on Good Friday. They are sweet buns with white icing crosses on top.

Family members get together to share an Easter dinner.

Easter Parades

In spring, Earth changes colors. People used to buy new, colorful clothes to celebrate. They showed off their new clothes by walking around town after Easter church services. This was how the Easter parade began.

Easter bonnets are the main attraction in the New York City Easter parade!

DID YOU KNOW?

There are no floats in the annual New York City Easter parade. Instead, people wear Easter bonnets and walk along Fifth Avenue.

In South America, people celebrate Holy Week, or Semana Santa, with parades. During these parades people carry crosses and act out Jesus' story.

Songs for Easter

People enjoy special music during Easter. The joyous songs celebrate the holiday. Many of the songs are **hymns**. During Easter church services, many people sing "Christ the Lord is Risen Today." The hymn is almost 300 years old.

Christians sing Easter hymns in church.

DID YOU KNOW?

The Easter song, "Peter Cottontail," was written in 1949. It was featured on a television special based on the novel, The Easter Bunny that Overslept.

Irving Berlin's song, "Easter Parade," was later used in a musical film titled *Easter Parade*.

American songwriter Irving Berlin wrote the song, "Easter Parade," in 1933. It tells the story of a young man and his girlfriend. They go to the Easter parade to show off her bonnet.

29

Around the World

People all over the world celebrate Easter. Different countries have different traditions. In Sweden, the Thursday before Easter is fun. Children dress up as witches. Then they go door-to-door asking for treats or money. People also put on plays for Easter. Passion plays teach people about Jesus' life during Holy Week. Many people still watch Passion plays at Easter.

DID YOU KNOW?

Instead of an Easter Bunny, Australians have an Easter Bilby. A bilby is about the size of a rabbit, but female bilbies have a pouch, like a kangaroo.

Actors perform Jesus' life, death, and resurrection in Passion plays.

Glossary

Christian Someone who believes that Jesus Christ is the Son of God

crucify Put to death by nailing the hands and feet to a cross

culture The customs of a group of people

disciple A person who followed Jesus and helped him teach people about God

hymn A religious song

Passover A religious holiday with a special meal that is celebrated by Jewish people

religious To believe in God

resurrected Brought back to life after death

sacrificed To give something as a gift to God

sin To break one of God's laws

symbol Something that stands for something else

tradition Custom or belief handed down from one generation to another

visually-challenged Unable to see well

Index

32

Printed in the U.S.A.—CG